the plantastic
cookbook

Gwen Kenneally

huquapress

Book written by Gwen Kenneally
Illustrations: Yoko Matsuoka
Art Direction: Judith A. Proffer
Design: designSimple

Published by IPG
814 North Franklin Street
Chicago, Illinois 60610
ISBN 978-1-957317-09-0
Printed in the United States of America

For Jack and Kay Kenneally

*Together again with the best seats in the
house to all 49er and Giants games. Forever
showing up in the invisible for all your children and
grandchildren. I am so grateful and humbled to
have chosen you to be my parents. There
are no words to express the love I feel
for you. Fly free with the angels.*

Table of Contents

Introduction

I have been tinkering with plant-based foods for decades. To begin with, I have always loved vegetables. I even have a nice vegetable garden growing on a small but mighty patch of land in my heart-of-Los Angeles home. But when my now-grown daughter claimed as a little girl that she was *never* (*ever*) going to eat animals again I really had to step up my game. I was determined that Emma would be nourished while eating food that looked and tasted good, all the while appealing to her little-kid sensibilities. And if you know me, you know that absolutely nothing comes out of my kitchen unless it tastes great, no matter how good it is for you.

We all know that eating a diet that leans plant-based is beneficial to our health as well as to the health of our planet. I for one am a happy girl pulling veggies from my garden and eating them fresh from the earth. I can eat vegetables all day long. I am the same with fruit. Yet I don't want to live without baked goods, cheese and a burger. So, I embarked on a quest to create satisfying and pretty plant-based recipes for my family and for my clients. It wasn't always pretty. And it wasn't always satisfying. When I was first enlisted to create a vegan dessert spread many (many) years ago I overheard a guest say that one of the cookies tasted like cardboard. Ouch. I saw another take a bite, and toss the rest in the trash. Ouch again. And then a little kid said, "Mommy, this cookie is gross!" I knew I needed to really figure this one out. There were not the resources, recipes, or information that exist today so I went around and around with flax seed, jackfruit, tofu, almond milk, and so many other plant-based foods to create foods that delivered on flavor, texture and visuals. Once I nailed the sweets, I moved on to more complex party fare. I did a vegan cocktail party where I prepared a vegan cheese board. Today I offer spectacular vegan and gluten-free blueberry pancakes at catered breakfasts. And my beloved grill still gets an amazing work out. My plant-based baked goods recipes are so good that many times guests enjoy without knowing the delicious thing they sampled was completely of the earth. No more gross cardboard with a spit-take. I was on my way.

So then it became my singular mission to recreate classic dishes, all plant-based, and to create brand new ones. I had many epic fails, and then I started to come up with recipes that were mega-hits and have become staples for my vegan and non-vegan clients. It's a joy to really deliver for my vegan clients, and to surprise those new to vegan eating with flavors and textures that dazzle and defy their expectations of what plant-based foods should look and taste like.

When my dear friend and publisher Judy Proffer conjured this book in a dream and asked if I would create a collection of my best plant-based recipes, I was thrilled to oblige. She said, "It will be part of our planet's healing. We need to eat more of what the earth offers us, not take without asking." All the recipes in this collection are made with ingredients that are easy to find in most markets. If something seems unfamiliar to you, ask your friendly grocery clerk.

These recipes are all about simple, good classic foods. They've all become a staple in my catering business, from backyard weddings to fancy parties to movie sets... and everything in between. I hope you have a Plantastic journey while bringing more delicious and nutritious plant-based foods into your world.

Toast Is My Jam

Cinnamon Nutzo Seven-Seed and Nut Butter Toast

2 slices whole-grain bread

6 tablespoons Nutzo Butter

Ground cinnamon

Toast the bread and spread 3 tablespoons
Nutzo over each slice. Sprinkle with
cinnamon. Serves 2.

Fava Bean Mint Toast

2 slices crusty bread

2 pounds fava beans

⅓ cup extra virgin olive oil

½ teaspoon salt, plus more for
sprinkling

½ cup mint leaves

Juice of 1 lemon

Freshly ground pepper

Sprinkle of arugula leaves

Heat a medium pot of water to boiling; blanch shelled fava beans in the boiling water for 2 or 3 minutes. Remove with a slotted spoon and transfer to an ice bath (bowl of water with ice) to cool rapidly. When cool, use a paring knife to slice open the skin and slip the inner beans out. You should have roughly a pound. In a food processor, place the shelled, blanched, cooled and skinned fava beans, olive oil, salt, mint leaves, lemon juice, and several rounds of freshly ground pepper. Puree until chunky but smooth. Meanwhile, toast the bread. Spread mixture evenly over both slices of toast. Sprinkle with arugula. Serves 2.

Pesto Avocado Toast

¼ cup pine nuts

2 large ripe avocados

2 cloves garlic

2 tablespoons lemon juice

1 cup packed fresh basil leaves

Salt, red pepper flakes, black pepper, to taste

4 slices whole-grain bread

Pit and halve the avocados and scoop the insides into the bowl of a food processor. Add the garlic, lemon juice, and salt. Blend until smooth. Add pine nuts and basil leaves, and pulse until the pine nuts and basil are broken down into very small pieces and the mixture is thoroughly blended. Toast the bread, and spread a generous amount of avocado pesto over each slice. Sprinkle lightly with freshly ground black pepper, red pepper flakes, and salt, to taste. Serve immediately. Serves 2 to 4.

Strawberry Ricotta Toast with Sweet Dukkah

1 pint strawberries, sliced

Vegan Ricotta

Sweet Dukkah

4 slices whole-grain crusty bread

Toast bread then spread a generous amount of ricotta over each slice. Add the strawberry slices and sprinkle with sweet dukkah. Serves 2 to 4.

Vegan Ricotta

2 cups cashews, soaked in water overnight

4 teaspoons nutritional yeast

2 tablespoons lemon juice

1 teaspoon sea salt

¾ to 1 cup water

Add all ingredients to a high-speed blender starting with ¾ cup water, adding more as needed. Blend until smooth. Put unused ricotta in a Mason jar and it will last for 5 days.

Sweet Dukkah

½ cup almonds, finely chopped

¼ cup hemp seeds

¼ cup pistachios, finely chopped

2 tablespoons chia seeds

2 tablespoons sesame seeds

2 tablespoons cinnamon

Pinch of salt

2 tablespoons olive oil

3 tablespoons honey

Preheat oven to 200°F. Line a baking tray with parchment paper. Combine seeds, nuts and spices, and spread on the tray. Drizzle with a little olive oil and toast for 5 minutes. Add honey and stir to combine. Toast for another 7 minutes until golden. Cool completely, then pulse in a food processor until roughly chopped. Put unused dukkah in a Mason jar and it will last for a month.

Vegan Farmer's Cheese with Raspberry, Mint and Hot Honey

1 pint fresh raspberries, sliced in half

4 ounces vegan farmer's cheese

10 fresh mint leaves

Hot honey

To make hot honey, place 1 cup honey and 2 teaspoons of any hot sauce of your choice in a small saucepan over low heat, stirring occasionally. Use while warm or place in a jar to use within the month. Spicy, sweet and sticky, this trendy honey update can be used to dress biscuits, fruit and even pizza.

Spread the cheese on the toast and arrange the sliced raspberries on top. Arrange the mint leaves on top. Drizzle with the hot honey and serve immediately.

Vegan Hazelnut Cocoa Spread with Dark Pink Himalayan Salt

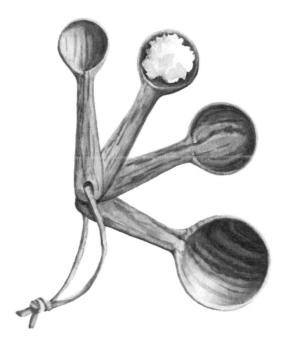

4 slices whole-grain bread

8 tablespoons hazelnut cocoa spread

Dark pink Himalayan salt

Toast bread and smear 2 tablespoons of the hazelnut cocoa spread over each piece. Sprinkle with salt and serve. Serves 2 to 4.

Vegan Hazelnut Cocoa Spread

3 cups raw unsalted hazelnuts

2 teaspoons vanilla extract

½ teaspoon sea salt

1 cup dairy-free dark chocolate

Preheat oven to 350°F and add hazelnuts to a baking sheet in a single layer. Roast for 12 to 15 minutes. Remove from oven and let cool slightly. Then transfer to a large kitchen towel and use your hands to roll the nuts around and remove most of the skins. Remove as much skin as possible to yield a creamier spread. Add hazelnuts to a food processor fitted with a steel blade. Blend on low until a butter consistency is formed, about 4 minutes, scraping down sides as needed. In the meantime, melt the chocolate over a double boiler. Set aside. Once the hazelnut butter is creamy and smooth, add the vanilla and salt and blend well. Then add melted chocolate a little at a time and blend again until well incorporated. Transfer to a clean jar and store at room temperature for 2-3 weeks.

Avocado Toast

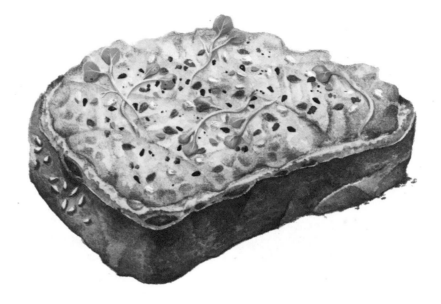

1 slice thick crusty bread

1 ripe avocado, peeled and seeded

Squeeze of lemon

Pinch of chili lime salt, to taste

Sprinkle of microgreens

In a work bowl, mash avocado and add squeeze of lemon and chili lime salt. Mix together, leaving a bit chunky. You want to achieve a perfect blend of creamy and chunky, so aim for that combination. Toast bread and spread avocado mixture generously. Sprinkle with microgreens. Serves 1 and can be easily doubled for 2 or made in bulk for a crowd.

Strawberry Rhubarb Jam

8 cups rhubarb, sliced

8 cups fresh or frozen strawberries, stems removed and cut in half

4 cups sugar

½ cup freshly squeezed lemon juice

1 teaspoon salt

1 teaspoon vanilla extract

1 teaspoon almond extract

Put the pieces of rhubarb and strawberries in a large heavy-bottom saucepan. Add the sugar, lemon juice, salt and stir to combine. Bring to a boil over medium heat, stirring occasionally. Once the jam begins to boil, partially cover the pan, adjusting the lid so that it covers about 80% of the pan. Adjust the heat as necessary to maintain a gentle simmer. Cook the jam for at least 1 hour, and up to 2 hours. Be cautious as you stir; as the jam begins to thicken, it will splatter. When the jam has thickened add vanilla and almond extract. Allow the jam to cool completely, then pour into 3 Mason pint jars. It will last in the refrigerator about 1 month.

Simple Mix-Berry Jam

12 cups berries (combination of blackberries, blueberries, raspberries, and hulled and roughly chopped strawberries)

1½ cups sugar

Juice and zest of 2 lemons

Prepare 2 sterilized pint-size Mason jars with lids. In a large nonreactive saucepan add the berries, sugar, and lemon zest and juice. Bring to a simmer, allowing the berries to soften, about 5 minutes. Mash the berries using a wooden spoon. Simmer until thickened and the sugar has completely dissolved, about 12 to 15 minutes. Pour into jars, leaving the top ¼ of the jars empty. Secure the lids and allow to cool to room temperature. Refrigerate overnight. Jam will last for about 2 weeks.

Lemon Curd

1 cup sugar

2 tablespoons cornstarch

1 cup non-dairy milk (oat or almond)

1 cup fresh lemon juice (from about 6 lemons)

1 teaspoon turmeric

6 teaspoons lemon zest (from about 5 lemons)

In a small pot, whisk together the sugar and cornstarch. Mix in the non-dairy milk, lemon juice, lemon zest, and turmeric. Put over medium heat, whisking frequently, until the curd thickens, about 5 minutes. You may need to whisk vigorously as it thickens to ensure a smooth curd. Remove from heat and pour into 2 Mason jars to cool. Store in the fridge for up to 1 week. It will thicken more as it cools. Makes 2 pints.

Soups & Stews

Beet Soup with Cashew Crème Fraîche

5 pounds large beets, peeled and cut into 2-inch chunks

2 onions, diced

1 leek, diced

6 tablespoons olive oil

¼ cup maple syrup

Salt and pepper

10 cups vegetable stock

Sauté onions and leeks in olive oil over medium heat. When vegetables begin to caramelize add maple syrup and beets. Cook until syrup bubbles. Add vegetable stock and simmer until beets are very tender. Add water if liquid reduces too much. Season to taste. Let soup cool slightly and then puree in blender. When ready to serve re-warm in a pot. Pour into 10 soup bowls. Place cashew crème fraîche in a squirt bottle. Squeeze out over the soup in the shape of hearts. Serves 8.

Cashew Crème Fraîche

1 cup raw cashews

¼ teaspoon salt

¼ cup cold water

2 teaspoons apple cider vinegar

2 tablespoons lemon juice

Cover cashews with water and soak overnight. Pour off all water, and place nuts in food processor. Add cold water, salt, vinegar, and lemon juice. Puree for 5 minutes or until completely smooth and creamy in consistency. Refrigerate in an airtight container for up to a week.

Citrus Gazpacho with Tortilla Chips

4 pounds heirloom tomatoes, peeled, seeded

2 cups orange juice

1 orange, peeled, segmented, diced

1 pink grapefruit, peeled, segmented, diced

3 garlic cloves, minced

1 tablespoon white wine vinegar

1 teaspoon salt

1 teaspoon orange zest

1 teaspoon lemon zest

1 tablespoon olive oil

1 cucumber, peeled, seeded, diced

1 cup red onion, diced fine

1 yellow bell pepper, diced

1 red pepper, diced

Black pepper, to taste

Cayenne pepper, to taste

Dice 1 tomato and reserve others for blending. Place reserved tomatoes, orange juice, and garlic in blender. Blend to a puree. Transfer puree to serving bowl. Add the vinegar, salt, olive oil, zest, diced orange, grapefruit, cucumbers, peppers, onion, diced tomato and black pepper. Mix well. Season with cayenne pepper to taste. Chill for at least 3 hours or overnight. Serves 4.

For the Chips

12 count package of corn tortillas

Peanut or sunflower oil for frying

Kosher salt

Preheat oil in deep skillet. On a cutting board stack 4 tortillas and cut into 8 wedges. Repeat with remaining tortillas. Add a handful of wedges to the hot oil. Separate any that stick together. Fry until golden brown. Remove and drain on a cookie sheet lined with a brown paper bag or paper towels. Sprinkle with salt and continue with the remaining tortillas.

Party Miso Soup

8 cups water

1 inch fresh ginger, finely chopped

1 cup Shiro miso (a fermented
   soybean paste)

Bunch of scallions, thinly sliced

1 cup firm tofu, chopped in
   ¼-inch cubes

Bring 7½ cups of water and ginger to a
boil. Whisk miso and ½ cup water in a
small bowl until smooth and whisk into
soup. Add tofu and scallions and simmer
for a few minutes before serving.
Serves 8 to 10.

Crowd-Pleasing Minestrone

2 tablespoons olive oil

2 yellow onions, diced

6 stalks celery (including leaves),
   thinly sliced

3 carrots, chopped

1 tablespoon Italian herbs
   (dried blend of oregano, parsley,
   basil, rosemary, thyme)

Sauté above ingredients over medium heat in large soup pot, then cover to sweat for 5 minutes.

Uncover and add:
   4 cloves garlic, minced

Sauté 5 more minutes, then add:
   12 cups vegetable stock

   3 cups canned or boxed tomatoes

   2 Yukon Gold potatoes, diced

   2 (15-ounce) cans cannellini beans,
      drained

   1 small head Savoy cabbage,
      quartered and sliced

Bring to boil and simmer 30 minutes.
Then add:
   8 ounces pasta of your choice

   6 more cups vegetable broth

   2 cups green beans, cut into
      1-inch pieces

Simmer 15 minutes. Serve with freshly grated vegan Parmesan cheese. Serves 12.

Vegan Parmesan Cheese

   ¼ cup nutritional yeast

   ½ cup hemp seeds

   ½ teaspoon garlic powder

   ½ teaspoon onion powder

   ¼ teaspoon fine sea salt, to taste

In a small bowl mix all ingredients together. Store this vegan Parmesan cheese in an airtight container at room temperature for up to 3 months.

Roasted Carrot, Asparagus, and Ginger Soup

1 tablespoon olive oil

2 medium red onions, sliced

1 (4-inch) piece fresh ginger, peeled

6 cloves garlic, peeled

8 cups vegetable stock

2 pounds carrots

2 pounds asparagus

Pinch of kosher salt

½ teaspoon white pepper

Roughly chop the carrots, asparagus, red onions, peeled ginger, and garlic. Toss with olive oil and place on sheet pan. Sprinkle with salt and pepper and roast for about 1 hour until tender. Move to soup pot and add the stock. Simmer over medium heat until the carrots are tender. Puree and season with salt and pepper. Serves 4 to 6.

Curry Zucchini Soup

2 pounds zucchini, diced

6 green onions, sliced

4 cups vegetable stock

2 tablespoons vegan butter or olive oil

1 teaspoon garam masala

½ teaspoon turmeric

¼ teaspoon cayenne pepper

Salt and pepper, to taste

In a large stockpot, sauté the zucchini and green onions for 5 minutes over medium heat. Add the remaining ingredients. Simmer for 30 minutes. Puree in batches and return to the pan and heat through. Serves 4 to 6.

Curried Red Pepper Soup

4 large red bell peppers, chopped

2 medium onion, chopped

4 tablespoons vegan butter

6 cups vegetable stock

2 cups vegan sour cream

1 teaspoon curry powder

Pepper, to taste

Sauté onion and pepper in butter over medium heat. When peppers are soft, add the curry powder and stock and cover. Once the peppers are soft, add cream, and puree. Return to low heat and simmer uncovered until a rich soupy consistency is attained. Add freshly ground black pepper to taste. Serves 4 to 6.

Spicy Red Lentil Soup

1 tablespoon olive oil

2 medium onions, chopped

3 cloves garlic, crushed

2 teaspoons ground cumin

2 teaspoons curry powder

¼ cup tomato paste

2 (15-ounce) cans crushed tomatoes

6 cups vegetable stock

½ cup red lentils

Heat oil in large pan, add onions and garlic, and cook over medium heat, stirring, until onions are soft. Add the rest of the ingredients and cook, uncovered, about 20 minutes or until lentils are tender. Serves 6 to 8.

Vegan Sausage and Grits

½ cup white beans

1 tablespoon nutritional yeast

1½ teaspoons garlic powder

1½ teaspoons onion powder

½ teaspoon each dried basil, rosemary, thyme, and oregano

½ to 2 teaspoons smoked paprika, to taste

3 tablespoons Bragg Liquid Aminos

1 tablespoon tamari or soy sauce

1 tablespoon fennel seeds

2 tablespoons maple syrup

½ cup vegetable stock

1¼ cups vital wheat gluten flour

In a bowl mix white beans with seasonings, then add the vegetable broth. Taste and adjust the seasonings as desired. Add the vital wheat gluten and knead into a ball. Split into 6 equal parts. Prepare 6 sheets of foil about 4 inches long. Shape each ball into a sausage and tightly wrap into the foil, twisting each end like a candy wrapper. Place in a steamer basket and steam for 45 minutes. Remove from the basket and let cool. Place in the refrigerator for at least 4 hours (or overnight). Warm in a skillet or grill and slice over the grits. Or you can place whole on a bun and eat like a sausage sandwich. Serves 6.

Vegan Grits

6 cups water

1 teaspoon salt

2 cups corn grits

3 tablespoons vegan butter

2 cups dairy-free cheese

Almond or hemp milk

Black pepper, to taste

To prepare the grits, bring the water and salt to boil. Whisk in the grits or cornmeal. Reduce heat to medium-low. Cook, stirring constantly, for 5 to 10 minutes, or until the grits are thick and creamy (cooking time will vary depending on the type of grits you use, so it's a good idea to check the package for instructions). Stir in vegan butter and the dairy-free cheese and black pepper. Add a splash of non-dairy milk for desired creaminess.

Place ¾ cup grits in each of 8 bowls. Top with sliced vegan sausage and sautéed spinach. Serves 8.

Sautéed Spinach

3 pounds baby spinach leaves

2 tablespoons olive oil

2 tablespoons chopped garlic (6 cloves)

Salt, to taste

Freshly ground black pepper, to taste

Rinse the spinach well in cold water to make sure it's very clean. Spin it dry in a salad spinner, leaving just a little water clinging to the leaves. In a large pot heat the olive oil and sauté the garlic over medium heat for about 1 minute, but not until it's browned. Add spinach, salt, and pepper to the pot, toss it with the garlic and oil, cover and cook for 2 minutes. Uncover the pot, turn the heat on high, and cook the spinach for another minute, stirring with a wooden spoon, until all the spinach is wilted. Serves 8.

Lentil Stew

½ cup olive oil

6 cloves garlic

1 cup chopped onion

1 cup diced carrots

1 cup chopped broccoli

1 cup kale

1 cup spinach

2 cups small green lentils

4 cups vegetable stock

4 cups marinara sauce

½ cup red wine

Salt and pepper, to taste

2 tablespoons basil

2 tablespoons thyme

1 Bouquet Garni

In a large soup pot, heat oil and sauté onions and garlic over medium heat. Add lentils, carrots, broccoli, kale, and spinach. Add the rest of the ingredients and cook over low heat for about 1 hour. Serves 6.

Bouquet Garni

Small bunch of parsley

8 sprigs thyme

8 sage leaves

2 bay leaves

Make a little herb packet by wrapping in a small piece of cheesecloth and securing by tying with a piece of kitchen string. This prevents the herbs from floating around and makes it easy to remove at the end. The bouquet garni can be varied to suit your dish or taste. I tend to use peppercorns, rosemary, whole cloves, whole nutmeg, dill, garlic, peels of lemon, limes and oranges.

Black-Eyed Peas for Prosperity and Smothered Greens

1 cup olive oil

2 large onions, chopped

6 large garlic cloves, minced

1 pound black-eyed peas, soaked in water overnight

4 pounds collard greens, stemmed, washed well and chopped or cut in ribbons

10 cups vegetable stock

1 teaspoon smoked paprika

½ cup organic tamari

½ cup Bragg Liquid Aminos

Cayenne pepper, to taste

Salt and freshly ground pepper, to taste

In a large pot over medium-high heat sauté the onions until caramelized. Add the garlic and stir for a moment longer; add soaked black-eyed peas and stir for another few minutes. Add the stock and bring to a boil. Reduce heat and cook for another 45 minutes, until the peas are tender, adding a bit of stock if the beans become too dry. Add the greens and all of the seasonings. Taste and adjust the seasoning as needed. Serve over Southern rice. Serves 4 to 6.

Southern Rice

6 tablespoons non-dairy butter
   or spread

2 cups sliced celery

2 cups sliced green onions

3 sliced green peppers

4 cups vegetable stock

½ teaspoon dried sage

½ teaspoon dried thyme

½ teaspoon rosemary

Salt and pepper, to taste

3 cups long-grain rice, uncooked

Coat a large skillet with vegan cooking spray. Add non-dairy butter or spread; place over medium heat until it melts. Add celery, green onions, and green peppers; sauté until crisp-tender. Stir in stock and add seasoning, salt and pepper. Bring to a boil.

In a 4-quart covered baking dish add rice on bottom; spoon the hot mixture over the rice, covering rice evenly with the vegetables. Cover and bake at 350°F for 30 minutes.

Note: for an alternative to rice in this dish, you can make a quick and easy cauliflower rice. To prepare the cauliflower rice, simply take 1 head of cauliflower, break into florets and pulse in a food processor until rice texture is achieved. Add 1 tablespoon of olive oil to a large skillet and sauté the cauliflower rice for 10 minutes until rice-like and golden.

Vegan Louisiana Red Beans and Rice

2 pounds red beans

½ cup olive oil

2 large onions, diced

10 cloves garlic

6 medium green peppers, chopped

6 stalks celery, chopped

5 bay leaves

6 chipotle peppers (from canned chipotles in adobo), finely chopped

½ teaspoon cayenne pepper

1 teaspoon smoked paprika

10 cups vegetable stock

½ cup chopped scallions, for garnish

Cooked rice, for serving

Tabasco sauce, for serving

Soak the beans overnight. Drain and set aside. Heat the olive oil over medium heat in a large heavy pot. Add the onion and caramelize. Add the garlic, peppers, and celery. Sauté until soft, about 5 or 6 minutes. Add the beans, bay leaves and chipotles, cayenne, smoked paprika, and vegetable stock. Bring to a boil, then reduce the heat and simmer, uncovered, until the beans are tender, about 1 hour. Add more water as needed to keep the beans from drying out. Mash a cup of the beans and stir back in to get it nice and thick. Serve with Mahatma rice. Serves 8.

Vegetable *Paella*

½ cup water

Large pinch of saffron

¼ cup extra virgin olive oil

2 red onions, diced

1 each red, yellow, and green bell peppers

6 garlic cloves, crushed

Bunch flat-leaf parsley leaves, chopped; reserve some for garnish

2 cups green beans, cut into 1-inch pieces

2 cups frozen or canned artichoke hearts

1 teaspoon smoked paprika

¼ to ½ teaspoon cayenne pepper

1 teaspoon salt

2 (15-ounce) cans whole tomatoes, drained and hand-crushed

8 cups short-grain Spanish rice

10 cups vegetable stock, warm

Generous pinch saffron threads

1 cup sweet peas, fresh or frozen and thawed

1 cup kidney beans

1 cup garbanzo beans

Lemon wedges, for serving

Bring water to a boil in small saucepan. Add saffron, cover and remove from heat. Let stand 10 minutes. Heat the oil in a paella pan and make a sofrito by sautéing the onions, garlic, and parsley. Cook for 10 minutes on a medium heat. Add the peppers and green beans and sauté for a few minutes longer. Then, add tomatoes and cook until the mixture caramelizes a bit and the flavors meld. Fold in the rice and stir-fry to coat the grains. Pour in vegetable stock, saffron water, salt, paprika, and cayenne pepper; simmer for 10 minutes, gently moving the pan around so the rice cooks evenly and absorbs the liquid. Add the beans and peas. Give the paella a good shake and let it simmer, without stirring, until the rice is al dente, about 15 minutes. When the paella is cooked and the rice looks fluffy and moist, turn the heat up for 40 seconds until you can smell the rice toast at the bottom, then it's perfect. The ideal paella has a toasted rice bottom called socarrat. Remove from heat and rest for 5 minutes. Garnish with parsley and lemon wedges. Serves 8 to 10.

Greens, Slaws & Salad

Kale and Blueberry Slaw

Dressing

1 cup balsamic vinegar

½ cup apple cider vinegar

¼ cup agave nectar

1 cup extra virgin olive oil

1 teaspoon dried thyme

1 cup blueberries

Sea salt, to taste

Place the dressing ingredients in a blender and blend until smooth. Place the kale in a large salad bowl, drizzle a tablespoon or so dressing over it, and give it a good massage. Once the kale is broken down, toss together the rest of the slaw ingredients, adding the rest of the dressing. Let sit for about 15 minutes before serving. Serves 4 to 6.

4 large bunches kale, washed and dried well, torn into bite-sized pieces

4 cups fresh blueberries

2 cups grated carrots

2 cups grated golden beets

8 shallots, thinly sliced

4 cups dried blueberries

4 cups sliced almonds

Wasabi Coleslaw

5 cups thinly sliced red and green
cabbage

1 cup vegenaise

3 to 8 teaspoons wasabi paste

4 tablespoons rice vinegar

Mix together cabbage, wasabi (add small
amounts at a time, tasting along the way
to reach your heat preference), vegenaise,
and vinegar in medium bowl. Chill for 2
hours or overnight. Serves 4 to 6.

Lentil, Fennel, and Roast Beet Salad

3 cups dry green lentils

4 cups water

1 large onion, chopped

2 garlic cloves, peeled and smashed

1 medium carrot, cut into 2 pieces

1 celery stalk, cut into 2 pieces

2 bay leaves

6 green onions, white and green parts, thinly sliced

1 small fennel bulb, thinly sliced

4 roasted beets, diced

Lemon Shallot French Dressing (recipe follows)

Salt

Freshly ground pepper

¼ cup minced parsley

Put the lentils into a large saucepan. Add water to cover, plus 3 inches. Bring to the boiling point and lower heat to very low. Add the onion, garlic, carrot, celery, and bay leaves. Simmer covered for about 30 minutes or until the lentils are tender but not mushy; they must retain their shape. Drain the lentils and remove the vegetables. Turn the lentils in to a bowl while they are still hot. Add the green onions, fennel, and roasted beets. Add the French dressing and mix well. Taste, then season with salt and pepper. Cool the lentils then cover the bowl and refrigerate for 2 hours to blend the flavors. At serving time, drain off any excess dressing. Place on a flat serving dish and garnish with the parsley. Serves 6.

Lemon Shallot French Dressing

⅓ cup olive oil

Juice of 2 large lemons

3 garlic cloves, minced

1 shallot, minced

¼ teaspoon dried thyme

Salt and pepper, to taste

Whisk all ingredients together.

Red Lentil Salad

1 cup red lentils, cooked and chilled

1 cup brown rice, cooked

1 pint golden raspberries

2 blood oranges, peeled and roughly chopped

¼ cup parsley

½ cup green onions

Blood Orange Vinaigrette (recipe follows)

Toss all ingredients. Chill for at least 1 hour before serving. Serves 4.

Blood Orange Vinaigrette

2 tablespoons white wine vinegar

¼ cup blood orange juice

Zest from 1 blood orange

⅔ cup olive oil

1 clove garlic, finely chopped

1 tablespoon finely chopped shallots

2 teaspoons finely chopped fresh parsley

2 teaspoons finely chopped fresh chives

Salt and pepper, to taste

Whisk together vigorously. Keeps in the refrigerator for 1 month.

Vegan Caesar Salad

The traditional Caesar salad is made with eggs and anchovy paste. I use an avocado for creaminess and Kalamata olives for brine. And since romaine lettuce is traditional, I like to add a mixture of romaine for the crunch, spinach for the color and spiciness, butter leaf for the crisp texture, and radicchio for the color. Any hearty lettuce will work. Use about 1 cup per person.

1 avocado

2 tablespoons Dijon mustard

6 Kalamata olives

Juice of 1 large lemon

3 tablespoons balsamic vinegar

Up to 3 cloves garlic, to taste

1 cup olive oil

2 teaspoons thyme

Nutritional yeast

¼ cup roasted pumpkin seeds

8 cups greens (lettuces and spinach), chopped

In a blender mix the avocado, mustard, olives, lemon, balsamic vinegar, and garlic. In a steady stream add the olive oil. Hand-mix in the thyme. Fill a large salad bowl with lettuce. Mix in croutons (recipe follows) and then toss in the dressing. Go lightly, as the worst Caesars are the ones that are over-dressed. Taste as you go. Sprinkle with nutritional yeast and roasted pumpkin seeds. Serves 8.

Croutons

You can use any kind of vegan bread (even gluten-free), seasoning and oil. This is a fairly basic recipe and you can build on it and get creative (rosemary, garlic) to make your own signature crouton.

> **1 baguette**
> **Olive oil to coat**
> **Pinch of kosher salt**
> **Fresh ground pepper**

Slice baguettes into quarter-inch slices. Place in large bowl. Toss with oil until well coated. Add salt and pepper. Place on a cookie sheet in single-layer rows and bake at 350°F until golden brown, about 20 minutes.

Roasted Pumpkin Seeds

> **½ cup raw pumpkin seeds**
> **2 tablespoons olive oil**
> **Seasoning**

Preheat oven to 300°F. Toss raw pumpkin seeds in a bowl with olive oil and seasonings of your choice (salt, garlic salt, cinnamon, Old Bay, Cajun seasoning, etc.). Spread pumpkin seeds in a single layer on baking sheet. Bake for about 45 minutes, stirring occasionally, until golden brown.

Kale Peace Salad

1 cup kale, finely chopped

1 cup collard greens, finely chopped

½ cup Napa cabbage, finely chopped

½ cup red cabbage, finely chopped

¼ cup red onions, finely chopped

1 cup cooked black-eyed peas, chilled

½ cup raw almonds, finely chopped

2 cups dried cranberries

Mix ingredients.

Clementine Orange Vinaigrette

¼ cup clementine orange juice

Zest from two clementines

½ cup olive oil

½ cup balsamic vinegar

½ cup mint leaves, de-stemmed

Mix dressing ingredients in a blender.
Toss with salad, lightly coating.
Serves 4.

Cucumber Mint Salad

4 cups chopped cucumber (approximately 3 medium-sized cucumbers)

2 cups fresh mint leaves, de-stemmed

1 cup fresh cilantro, de-stemmed

1 cup lime juice

⅓ cup grapeseed oil

1 cup fresh yellow cherry tomatoes

Raw macadamia nuts, chopped

Fresh basil leaves pulled from stem

Combine all ingredients in a large bowl and serve. Serves 4.

Cucumber mint is one of the culinary world's freshest pairings. Toss both in a glass of water and you're treated to a perfectly refreshing sip of wonderful. This salad offers that same freshness with the added bonus of crunch and elevated flavor with cilantro, lime and basil.

Black Bean and Corn Salad

3 cups black beans (cooked al dente and drained)

3 cups roasted white corn (cooked al dente)

1 red onion, diced

1 red pepper, diced

1 cup cilantro, chopped

1 garlic clove, minced

1 jalapeño, minced

2 avocados, chopped (firm, not overly ripe)

½ cup olive oil

½ cup balsamic vinegar

⅓ cup of lime juice

4 cups arugula

Combine black beans, corn, red pepper, cilantro, jalapeño, and avocado.

Add olive oil, vinegar, and lime juice and mix together.

Place on a bed of arugula and serve. Serves 4 to 6.

Thai Mango Salad

2 heads butter leaf lettuce, chopped into bite-sized pieces

3 red bell peppers, thinly sliced, then sliced across to make 1-inch-long pieces

3 ripe mangos, diced

6 green onions, diced

⅓ cup almond slices (reserve small amount to sprinkle on top)

¼ cup chopped fresh cilantro

1 medium jalapeño, seeds and membranes removed, finely chopped

Almond Butter Dressing

½ cup creamy almond butter

½ cup lime juice (about 2 to 3 limes)

2 tablespoons tamari

2 tablespoons apple cider vinegar

1 tablespoon honey

2 teaspoons sesame oil

4 cloves garlic, minced

Pinch of red pepper flakes, to taste

Place all the salad ingredients in a large bowl. In a small bowl whisk together the almond butter dressing ingredients. Toss with the salad and sprinkle with reserved almonds. Serves 4.

Some of My Favorite Salad Dressings

Açai and Orange Dressing

½ cup açai juice

3 tablespoons orange juice

1½ tablespoons grated orange rind

3 tablespoons rice vinegar

1½ tablespoons grapeseed oil

¼ teaspoon crushed red pepper

Combine all ingredients in a small bowl, stirring well with a whisk.

Honey Mustard Dressing

1 cup plain cashew yogurt (recipe follows)

4 tablespoons Dijon mustard

2 tablespoons honey

2 tablespoons cider vinegar

Combine yogurt, honey, mustard and cider vinegar in a jar. Tighten lid and shake until blended. Chill 30 minutes before serving.

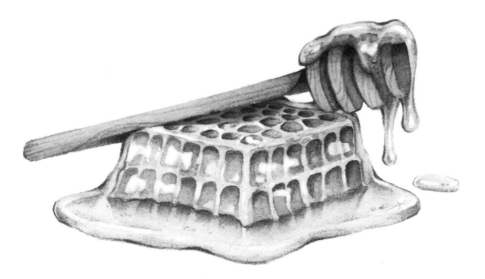

Cashew Yogurt

4 cups unsweetened almond milk

1 cup raw cashews, soaked in water overnight

3 tablespoons non-dairy yogurt

Place 1 cup almond milk and cashews in a blender and process on high until smooth and creamy. Transfer to a heavy saucepan and stir in the rest of the almond milk. Warm over low heat, whisking occasionally, until the mixture reaches 110°F. (If you don't have a thermometer, test a little on your wrist and when it feels warm, remove from heat.) Add the non-dairy yogurt and whisk until smooth. Place in a 1-quart jar and cover to let rest for 6 hours. Move to the refrigerator for up to 1 week.

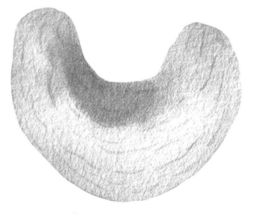

Peanut Wasabi Vinaigrette

¼ cup rice vinegar

¼ cup grapeseed oil

½ cup peanut or almond butter

3 tablespoons soy sauce

3 tablespoons wasabi paste

2 tablespoons minced fresh ginger

3 cloves fresh-minced garlic

Combine all ingredients, stirring well to combine. Let stand for 45 minutes.

Jackfruit of all Trades

Crabby Jack Cakes with Red Pepper Sauce

1 (20-ounce) can of jackfruit

1 flax egg (1 tablespoon ground
flaxseed mixed with 3 tablespoons
water)

1 small red onion, minced

1 red bell pepper, minced

1 cup panko bread crumbs

½ teaspoon salt

1 teaspoon dried mustard powder

¼ teaspoon cayenne pepper

1 teaspoon Old Bay seasoning

3 cups grapeseed oil (for frying)

Drain the jackfruit and place in a food
processor fitted with a steel S blade.
Quickly pulse the jackfruit until shredded.
Mix with all the other ingredients. Cover
and refrigerate for 2 hours. Shape the
mixture into 8 cakes. Pour grapeseed oil
in a heavy skillet. Fry the crab cakes over
medium heat for 5 minutes per side until
golden brown. Serve with red pepper
sauce. Serves 4-6.

Roasted Red Pepper Sauce

1 (16-ounce) jar of roasted red peppers

2 cups vegan mayonnaise

2 cloves garlic, chopped

1 bunch chives

Place everything but the chives
in a blender and mix until smooth.
Dice the chives finely and add to
the sauce.

Chinese Jack Salad with Toasted Almonds

For the dressing

In a small bowl whisk, together:

3 cloves garlic, finely chopped

1 inch ginger, peeled and finely chopped

1 cup peanut butter

¼ cup soy sauce

1 cup rice wine vinegar

1 tablespoon wasabi paste

3 tablespoons toasted sesame seeds

Crushed red pepper, to taste

In a slow steady stream add:
  ¼ cup sesame oil
  ½ cup sunflower oil

For the salad

1 (20-ounce) can jackfruit, shredded in food processor

4 cups white cabbage, shredded

4 cups red cabbage, shredded

4 cups kale

4 large carrots, peeled, grated

1 bunch scallions, thinly sliced on the diagonal

Toss together in a pretty salad bowl and massage the dressing into the salad until it is nicely dressed.

Then garnish with the following:
  ½ cup finely chopped cilantro
  1 cup almond slices

Fried Jackfruit

1 (20-ounce) can jackfruit in brine

Peanut or vegetable oil for frying

Breading

1 cup all-purpose flour

1½ teaspoons salt

1 teaspoon ground black pepper

½ teaspoon onion powder

1 teaspoon thyme

½ teaspoon ground ginger

½ teaspoon smoked paprika

½ teaspoon garlic powder

4 or 5 shakes of cayenne pepper, to taste

4 or 5 shakes of oregano, to taste

1 teaspoon red pepper flakes

Vegan buttermilk (1 cup almond or oat milk blended with 1½ teaspoons apple cider vinegar)

In a glass measuring cup, mix together the ingredients for the vegan buttermilk and set aside. In a medium-size bowl, mix the breading ingredients and set aside. Add enough oil to a frying pan to cover the pieces of jackfruit and turn on medium heat. Drain and rinse your jackfruit. On a cutting board, begin cutting parts of the jackfruit that are hard or contain seeds; you want to try and leave only the parts that are stringy or soft. Begin by dipping the jackfruit piece in the vegan buttermilk mixture, then transfer to the breading, then back in the vegan buttermilk, then in the breading again. Once completed, add it to the hot frying pan. You will know if they're ready when you touch them with your tongs and the outer breading is firm and crispy. Repeat until all jackfruit is fried. Once the jackfruit is fried, transfer to a plate with 3 or 4 layers of paper towels so that some of the oil can be absorbed. Allow them to cool for 5 minutes before serving. Serve with waffles and maple syrup.

Jackfruit "Chicken" and Waffles

For the Waffles

3 cups flour

2 tablespoons baking powder

1 to 2 tablespoons sugar

½ teaspoon salt

3 cups rice milk

⅓ cup orange juice

⅓ cup sunflower or vegetable oil

1 teaspoon vanilla extract

Cooking spray or cooking oil

Preheat waffle maker. In a medium bowl, mix together all the ingredients until smooth. Spray preheated waffle iron with non-stick cooking spray or lightly brush with oil. Pour batter onto waffle iron and cook until golden brown. Serve with fried jackfruit and maple syrup.

Jackfruit "Bacon"

1 (20-ounce) can green jackfruit, unsweetened

4 tablespoons liquid smoke

4 tablespoons coconut aminos

2 tablespoons olive oil

2 tablespoons maple syrup

2 teaspoons balsamic vinegar

2 teaspoons molasses

¼ to ½ teaspoon Himalayan pink salt

Preheat oven to 425°F. Line 2 large baking sheets with parchment paper. Drain and rinse the jackfruit. Dry between 2 clean towels. Slice thin, as evenly as possible. The jackfruit may become stringy or break apart, and that's okay. Set aside. In a medium bowl, mix together all the marinade ingredients. Whisk together until uniform, then toss in the jackfruit. Mix until all the jackfruit is coated. Cover the bowl and place into the refrigerator overnight. Remove from the refrigerator, and evenly distribute on the baking sheets. Save the remaining marinade for dressing or more bacon. Place in the oven for 20 to 25 minutes, flipping halfway through. In the final half, check up on it from time to time as it may burn easily. Remove from the oven and cool for 15 minutes. Enjoy or store in the refrigerator.

Jack Birria Street Tacos

Jackfruit

2 Cans (20 ounces) green jackfruit in brine, drained

1 yellow onion, peeled and quartered

1 head garlic

3 bay leaves

1 tablespoon salt

Shred the jackfruit in a food processor fitted with an S blade. Place in a medium pot and cover with water. Add the onion, garlic, bay leaves, and salt. Simmer slowly for 15 minutes. Remove from heat, drain, and let cool slightly. Squeeze all the water out with your hands or by placing it in a towel. Set aside.

Sauce

4 ancho and 4 guajillo chiles, dried, deseeded, destemmed

2 pasilla and 2 morita chiles, deseeded and destemmed

6 Roma tomatoes, medium

2 black peppercorns

2 cloves

1 teaspoon cumin seeds

1 stick Ceylon cinnamon (1 inch long)

1 teaspoon each dried thyme, oregano and marjoram

¼ cup apple cider vinegar

3 cups vegetable broth

Toast the peppercorns, cloves, cinnamon stick, and cumin seeds in a small sauté pan set to medium heat until fragrant. In a cast-iron skillet toast the chilies over medium heat for a couple of seconds on each side until they begin to change color. Place them in a pot and cover with water. Bring to a boil and turn the heat off. Let soak for 10 minutes. In the same cast-iron pan, char the tomatoes on both sides until they are slightly blackened. Place in a blender with the garlic and onion from the jackfruit. Add the marjoram, thyme, oregano, bay leaves, and apple cider vinegar to the blender. Drain the chilies, but reserve the liquid. Add the chilies to the blender and 1½ cups of the soaking liquid. Blend until smooth. If necessary add more liquid to get a smooth puree. Strain and set aside. Place oil in a large stockpot and sauté the jackfruit until golden brown. Lower heat, and pour in chile puree. Stir. Let simmer for 5 minutes, then add the vegetable stock. Bring to a simmer, and let cook for 30 minutes. Season to taste with salt and pepper. Serve with chopped cilantro, diced onion, and toasted tortillas. Serves 4 to 6.

Quinoa

Sunday Brunch Garbanzo Bean and Quinoa Cake Benedict with Hollandaise Sauce

For the Cake

1½ cups quinoa

3 cups vegetable stock

3 tablespoons flaxseed meal

9 tablespoons water

1 tablespoon thyme, divided

1 tablespoon oregano

Smoked paprika, to taste

Cayenne pepper, to taste

Salt and cracked pepper, to taste

3 (15-ounce) cans garbanzo beans, drained and rinsed

1½ cups corn

2 red bell peppers, finely diced

1 red onion, finely diced

Juice and zest of 1 lemon

1 cup oat flour

10 English muffins, toasted

In a medium pot, bring veggie stock, quinoa, and 1 teaspoon thyme to a hard boil. Give a good stir and cover; remove from heat and stir every 10 minutes until all the stock is absorbed. In a small bowl whisk together the flaxseed and water until thick. In a large bowl mash ¾ of the beans, leaving a quarter of the batch whole or somewhat whole. Add the quinoa to the beans along with the onions, red pepper, corn (I save a handful of each for garnish), remaining 2 teaspoons thyme, oregano, smoked paprika, cayenne pepper, lemon zest and juice. Mix well. Add in the flour and flaxseed mix and blend well. Season to taste with salt, pepper, and more of the other spices.

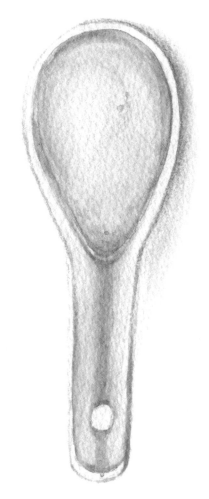

Now to divide into 20 balls and make your patties. Flatten with your palms and place on hard surface. Make them about ½-inch thick and about 3 inches around (the size of an English muffin). In a large skillet, heat 1 tablespoon olive oil over medium heat. Cook cakes about 4 or 5 minutes on each side. Serve 1 cake over an English muffin and plate 2 per person, cover with hollandaise sauce and garnish with the reserved vegetables and fresh thyme.

Hollandaise Sauce

- 1 cup vegan butter
- 6 tablespoons all-purpose flour
- Pinch of turmeric
- Pinch of smoked paprika
- Big pinch of cayenne pepper
- 2 tablespoons nutritional yeast
- 3 cups almond milk
- Zest and juice of 2 lemons
- 3 tablespoons vegenaise
- Salt and pepper, to taste

Heat a small saucepan over medium-low heat. Add the vegan butter and heat until it is sizzling and boiling quite a bit. Whisk in the flour all at once to make a paste and continue to whisk it constantly for about a minute. Add a very small pinch of turmeric. Slowly whisk in almond milk. Bring sauce to a boil, whisking frequently. Boil for 2 to 3 minutes and remove from heat. Whisk in the cayenne, smoked paprika, and nutritional yeast. Add the lemon juice and mix well. Season to your taste with salt and black pepper. Lastly, add the vegenaise for a little bit more creaminess.

Roasted Acorn Squash and Pears *with Quinoa, Fall Greens, and Pomegranate Ginger Vinaigrette*

2 tablespoons coconut oil

1 acorn squash, sliced in ½-inch-thick rounds and seeds removed

Salt and pepper, to taste

Red pepper flakes, to taste

2 teaspoons brown sugar

½ cup pecan pieces

¼ teaspoon pumpkin pie spice

6 cups fall greens, baby kale, and arugula

2 cups cooked red quinoa

1 ripe pear, sliced

1 avocado, sliced

1 cup pomegranate seeds

1 cucumber, sliced

Heat a large skillet over medium heat and add coconut oil. Toss the squash slices with salt, pepper, crushed red pepper, and brown sugar. Add them to the skillet and cook until golden, about 5 minutes per side. Heat a small saucepan over low heat and add the pecans. Toast until they are slightly golden and fragrant, stirring and shaking the pan as they toast, for about 5 minutes. Toss them with the pumpkin pie spice. In a large bowl add arugula, baby kale, and fall greens, and season with a pinch of salt and pepper. Add the pear slices, avocado, pomegranate seeds, cucumber, quinoa, and squash pieces. Toss with the pomegranate dressing and sprinkle with pecans. Serves 8 to 10.

Quinoa

1 cup red quinoa

2 cups vegetable stock or water

Place quinoa and water or vegetable stock in a saucepan. Bring to a hard boil uncovered. Give a good stir. Remove from heat and cover. Let sit for 20 minutes. Uncover and stir. Leave to cool. Makes about 2 cups.

Pomegranate Ginger Vinaigrette

⅓ cup pomegranate juice

¼ cup apple cider vinegar

½ teaspoon freshly grated ginger

⅓ cup olive oil

Salt and pepper, to taste

Combine pomegranate juice, vinegar, ginger, salt and pepper in a large bowl and whisk together. Stream in the olive oil while constantly whisking until the dressing comes together.

Breakfast Quinoa

2 cups quinoa

3 cups vegetable stock

1 cup onion, chopped

1 cup red bell pepper, chopped

1 cup candied ginger, chopped

2 cups dried fruit, chopped (an
assortment of apricots, cranberries,
cherries and blueberries works nicely)

1 cup sliced almonds

Mint for garnish

Mix together and toss with maple syrup
balsamic dressing (below). Garnish with
mint. Serves 6 to 8.

Maple Balsamic Vinaigrette

2 cloves garlic, finely chopped

2 tablespoons Dijon mustard

1 tablespoon maple syrup

6 tablespoons balsamic vinegar

1 cup olive oil

Fresh ground pepper

Whisk all ingredients together and let
stand for 1 hour.

Quinoa Salad

2 cups quinoa

4 cups vegetable stock

2 large tomatoes, chopped

1 large bunch chives, chopped

½ cup young mung bean sprouts

½ cup raw pine nuts

Dressing

⅓ cup olive oil or walnut oil

1 lime or Meyer lemon, juiced

2 cloves garlic, minced

Pinch sea salt

Bring quinoa and vegetable broth to a boil. Cover; reduce heat to simmer for 10 to 15 minutes. While quinoa is cooking, chop tomatoes and chives. Mix dressing. Remove quinoa from heat. Allow to cool. Fluff quinoa and add vegetables and pine nuts. Gently mix dressing into quinoa mixture. Serve cold or warm. Serves 6.

Quinoa Risotto

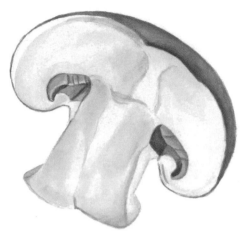

1 cup quinoa

1 tablespoon olive oil

1 cup chopped onion

3 cloves garlic, minced

1 cup vegetable broth

1 cup oat milk

8 ounces mushrooms, sliced

¾ cup nutritional yeast

3 tablespoons flaxseed

Rinse and drain quinoa 3 times, using a fine mesh strainer to remove the bitter outer coating. Heat olive oil in a heavy saucepan or Dutch oven over medium-high heat. Add onion and cook until soft, stirring constantly. Add garlic and quinoa and continue stirring for a minute or two. Stir in broth and oat milk. Bring to a boil, then reduce heat to low and simmer until quinoa is tender, stirring occasionally, approximately 10 to 12 minutes. Add mushrooms and cook another 3 to 5 minutes, stirring often. Remove from heat. Add nutritional yeast and flaxseed, give a quick stir and let stand a few minutes, so risotto can thicken. Serves 2.

Black Bean and Lime Quinoa

Juice and zest from 3 limes

2 tablespoons olive oil

1 tablespoon vegetable oil

1 cup quinoa

1 (14- to 15-ounce) can black beans, drained and rinsed

2 medium tomatoes, diced

4 scallions, chopped

3 cloves garlic

¼ cup chopped fresh cilantro

Salt and pepper, to taste

Whisk together lime zest and juice, oils, salt and pepper in a large bowl. Wash quinoa in 3 changes of cold water in a bowl, draining in a sieve each time. Cook quinoa in a medium pot of boiling salted water uncovered, until almost tender, about 10 minutes. Drain in sieve, then set sieve in same pot with 1 inch of simmering water (water should not touch bottom of sieve). Cover quinoa with a folded kitchen towel, then cover sieve with lid and steam over medium heat until tender, fluffy, and dry, about 10 minutes. Remove pot from heat and remove lid. Let stand, still covered with towel, 5 minutes. Serves 4 to 6.

Curried Quinoa

2 cups quinoa

4 cups water

½ cup slivered almonds, toasted

½ cup raisins

2 large tomatoes

4 carrots, grated

1 cup sweet peas

1 green bell pepper

4 teaspoons curry powder

2 teaspoons chili powder

1 teaspoon cumin

½ cup cilantro, chopped

Kosher salt

In a good-sized pot, sauté quinoa kernels in a little bit of olive oil about 4 minutes, then pour in water, cover, and let boil about 15 minutes until absorbed. Cut up veggies while you wait. When water is absorbed, fluff with a fork and add spices and all veggies except for shredded carrots and cilantro. After stirring a good 30 seconds on heat, remove, dish into bowls, and garnish with carrot and cilantro. Serves 4 to 6.

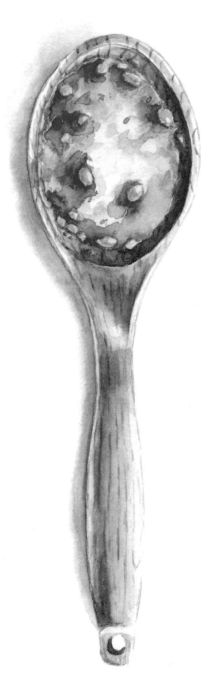

Quinoa Tabouli

2 cups quinoa, cooked

1 cup chopped parsley

½ cup chopped scallions

2 tablespoons mint

2 tablespoons chopped basil leaves

3 garlic cloves, minced

Juice of 1 lemon

¼ cup olive oil

Salt and pepper, to taste

¼ cup olives, sliced

Place all ingredients in a mixing bowl and toss together lightly. Chill for 1 hour or more to allow flavors to blend. Garnish with olives. Serves 4.

Seitan and Quinoa Salad

2 cups quinoa

4 cups vegetable stock

Salt, to taste

1 cup pine nuts, toasted

4 tablespoons red wine vinegar

Pepper, to taste

4 tablespoons olive oil

3 cups cooked seitan, finely chopped
(recipe follows)

1½ cups green and red grapes,
quartered

Bring stock to a boil. Stir quinoa and a
pinch of salt into water. Reduce heat,
cover and simmer for 15 to 20 minutes,
until quinoa is tender and all of the liquid
is absorbed. Uncover and let cool. Whisk
vinegar and oil. Add seitan, grapes, pine
nuts, and quinoa. Toss well and add salt
and pepper to taste. Serves 4.

Grilled Seitan

1 8-ounce piece of seitan

Poultry seasoning

2 tablespoons olive oil

Mix olive oil and poultry seasoning.
Add seitan and let marinate for 1
hour. Preheat grill to medium heat;
grill 4 to 5 minutes each side until
slightly charred.

Quinoa Burger

1½ cups cooked quinoa

1 cup hummus

2 tablespoons tomato paste

1 tablespoon sesame oil

1 tablespoon soy sauce

10 basil leaves, chopped

2 sprigs thyme, chopped

Pinch cayenne pepper, to taste

Salt and pepper, to taste

6 burger buns

Mixed greens to dress burger

Avjar Sauce (recipe follows)

Blend all ingredients in a bowl or food processor. Divide burger mix into 6 equal portions and form into 4-inch patties. Grill on medium heat 5 minutes each side, until browned and firm. Place patties on buns and top with avjar and mixed greens. Serves 6.

Homemade Avjar

8-12 fresh red paprika (mild or medium-hot, to taste)

4 medium-size eggplants

½ cup olive oil

1 large onion, minced

3 large garlic cloves, chopped

Juice of 1 lemon

¼ cup parsley leaves

Salt and pepper to taste

Roast the paprika and eggplants in a preheated 475 F oven until the skin is blistered and darkened, approximately thirty minutes. Remove from oven and place the now roasted vegetables in a paper bag and let them steam in their own heat for 10 minutes. Peel off and discard the burnt skin along with the stems and seeds. Mash the peppers and eggplant pulp together to form a slightly chunky mass. You can do this with a fork or in a food processor. Heat 3 tablespoons of oil in a large skillet and sauté the onion until very soft. Add garlic and cook for 2 more minutes. Remove from the heat and stir in the pepper and eggplant pulp, mixing well. Slowly drizzle the remaining oil into the mixture, stirring constantly to incorporate all of the oil. Add the lemon juice, parsley, and salt and pepper to taste.

Baked Quinoa Loaf *with* Roasted Beet Gravy

2 cups red quinoa, rinsed and drained

4 cups vegetable stock

2 (15.5-ounce) cans dark red kidney beans, drained and rinsed

2 cups roasted diced red beets plus 1 tablespoon beet cooking liquid

3 tablespoons ground golden flaxseed

½ cup water

1½ cups rolled oats

1½ cups ground cashews

1 teaspoon dried thyme

1 teaspoon dried oregano

1 teaspoon dried basil

1 teaspoon salt

½ teaspoon black pepper

1 teaspoon red pepper flakes, to taste

Combine the quinoa and vegetable stock in a medium saucepan and bring to a boil over high heat. Remove from heat, cover, and let sit for 30 minutes until the quinoa is tender and the water is absorbed. Preheat oven to 375°F.

Whisk together the flaxseed and water and let set for 5 minutes. Spray two 9-inch loaf pans. In a food processor, combine all of the ingredients except the cooked quinoa, and process to combine well. The mixture should be finely ground but with some texture remaining. Transfer the mixture to a bowl and add the reserved quinoa, stirring to mix well. Taste and adjust the seasonings as needed, then transfer the mixture evenly into the prepared pan and smooth the top. Bake until firm, about 45 minutes. Let the loaf cool for 10 to 15 minutes, then carefully turn out onto a plate by placing a plate over the loaf and inverting it so that the loaf is now on the plate and ready to serve. Serves 8 to 10.

Roasted Beet Gravy

- 6 cups roasted beets
- 1 cup cashews, soaked in water overnight
- 3 or 4 cups vegetable stock
- 2 to 4 tablespoons horseradish
- Salt and pepper, to taste
- Sage chiffonade

In a stockpot place beets, horseradish, and 3 cups of vegetable stock. Bring to a boil and pull from heat. Puree using an immersion blender (or let cool and use a traditional blender). Add the cashews and more stock as needed to get that lush gravy consistency. Return to a low simmer to reheat. Taste and adjust seasoning. Pour over the quinoa loaf and garnish with sage chiffonade.

Mix-Berry Quinoa Pudding

2 cups almond milk

1 cup quinoa

2 cups mixture blackberries, blueberries, strawberries, raspberries

½ teaspoon ground cinnamon

⅓ cup chopped pecans, toasted

4 teaspoons agave nectar

Combine almond milk and quinoa in a medium saucepan. Bring to a boil over high heat. Reduce heat to medium-low; cover and simmer 15 minutes or until most of the liquid is absorbed. Turn off heat; let stand covered 5 minutes. Stir in berries and cinnamon; transfer to 4 bowls and top with pecans. Drizzle 1 teaspoon agave nectar over each serving. Serves 4.

Quinoa Orange and Cranberry Cookies

1½ cups white whole wheat flour (rice flour or gluten-free are options)

1 teaspoon kosher salt

½ teaspoon baking powder

½ teaspoon baking soda

½ cup plant-based butter

¼ cup sugar

¼ cup packed light brown sugar

¼ cup maple syrup

2 flax eggs (each egg is 1 tablespoon ground flaxseed with 3 tablespoons water)

1 teaspoon vanilla

½ teaspoon almond extract

1 cup cooked quinoa, cooled

1 cup old-fashioned oats

1 cup dried cranberries (orange-flavored if you can find them)

Zest of 1 orange

½ cup slivered almonds

Preheat oven to 375°F. Line 2 baking sheets with parchment paper. Whisk flour, salt, baking powder, and baking soda in a medium bowl. Using an electric mixer beat butter, both sugars, and syrup in a large bowl until light and fluffy, about 3 minutes. Add flax eggs, almond extract, and vanilla and beat until pale and fluffy, about 2 minutes. Beat in flour mixture, ½ cup at a time. Stir in quinoa, oats, cranberries, orange zest, and almonds. Spoon dough in 2-tablespoon portions onto prepared sheets, spacing 1 inch apart. Bake cookies until golden, 12 to 15 minutes. Transfer cookies to a wire rack and let cool. Makes 4 dozen.

Grilled Sides & Entrees

Cedar-Planked Pecan, Bourbon and Brown Sugar Glazed Vegan Brie

Cedar grilling plank

½ cup packed dark brown sugar

¼ cup chopped pecans

2 tablespoons dried cherries

1 tablespoon bourbon

8-ounce round vegan Brie (recipe follows)

1 Granny Smith apple, cored and thinly sliced

1 pear, cored and thinly sliced

2 tablespoons lemon juice

Small bunch of grapes

Sourdough vegan baguette, thinly sliced on the diagonal

Soak the cedar plank in water for at least 30 minutes. If necessary, weigh it down to keep it submerged. Meanwhile, in a small bowl stir together the brown sugar, pecans, dried cherries, and bourbon. Heat the grill to indirect medium heat.

Place the Brie on the wet cedar plank. Place the plank on the grill and cook for 10 minutes, or until the Brie is slightly softened and the sugar melts. Meanwhile, in a medium bowl, toss the apple and pear slices with the lemon juice. Arrange bread, the slices of apples and pears, and grapes around the sides of the Brie. Serve on the plank with a cheese knife.

Brie Cheese

⟩ 2 cups raw cashews, soaked in water
   overnight

1 cup plain unsweetened non-dairy
   yogurt

1 cup refined coconut oil, melted

2 teaspoons nutritional yeast

1 teaspoon white miso

1 teaspoon salt

2 cups water

4 tablespoons tapioca starch

2 teaspoons kappa carrageenan

Add the cashews, yogurt, coconut oil, nutritional yeast, white miso, salt, and water to a blender. Blend until smooth. Transfer the "Brie" mixture to a large bowl, cover with a kitchen towel, and let sit at room temperature for 12 to 16 hours. Transfer the mixture to a large saucepan over medium-high heat and add tapioca starch and kappa carrageenan. Cook, whisking constantly, until the mixture is thick and pulls away from the sides of the pan, about 5 minutes. Line an 8- or 9-inch round with cheesecloth and pour in the hot cheese mixture. Cover with the cheesecloth. Let cool in the refrigerator until firm, 4 to 8 hours. When ready to eat, remove the cheesecloth. Store in the refrigerator for up to 3 days.

Grilled Artichokes

2 lemons

4 large artichokes (3 or 3½ pounds total)

1 tablespoon olive oil

Salt and pepper, to taste

To prepare artichokes: fill a stockpot with water; add the juice of 1 lemon. Trim leaves from the top of an artichoke. Remove the outer layer(s) of leaves from the stem end and snip all remaining spiky tips from the outer leaves. Trim an inch off the bottom of the stem and use a vegetable peeler to remove the fibrous outer layer. As each artichoke is prepared, drop it into the lemon water to prevent it from turning brown. When all the artichokes are prepared, cover the pan and bring to a boil. Boil until the base of the stem can be pierced with a fork, 12 to 15 minutes. Transfer to a cutting board and let stand until cool enough to handle, about 10 minutes.

Meanwhile, preheat grill to medium. Slice the artichokes in half lengthwise. Scoop out the choke and first few inner layers in the center until the bottom is revealed. Brush each half with oil and sprinkle with salt and pepper. Grill the artichokes until tender and lightly charred, about 5 minutes per side. Transfer to a serving platter, squeeze half a lemon over them, and garnish with the remaining lemon half cut into 4 wedges. Serve warm, at room temperature, or chilled. Serves 4 to 6.

Grilled Vegetable Platter

3 red bell peppers, seeded and halved

3 yellow squash, sliced lengthwise into ½-inch-thick rectangles

3 zucchini, sliced lengthwise into ½-inch-thick rectangles

3 Japanese eggplants, sliced lengthwise into ½-inch-thick rectangles

1 bunch (1 pound) asparagus, trimmed

12 green onions

Olive oil

Salt and pepper, to taste

3 tablespoons balsamic vinegar

2 garlic cloves, minced

1 teaspoon chopped fresh Italian parsley leaves

1 teaspoon chopped fresh basil leaves

Place a grill pan over medium-high heat or prepare the barbecue (medium-high heat). Brush the vegetables with oil to coat lightly. Sprinkle the vegetables with salt and pepper. Working in batches, grill the vegetables until tender and lightly charred all over, about 8 to 10 minutes for the bell peppers; 7 minutes for the yellow squash, zucchini, eggplant; 4 minutes for the asparagus and green onions. Arrange the vegetables on a platter. Meanwhile whisk 2 tablespoons of oil, balsamic vinegar, garlic, parsley, and basil in a small bowl to blend. Add salt and pepper to taste. Drizzle the herb mixture over the vegetables. Serves 10.

Vegetable Kebabs

2 zucchini, cut into 2-inch chunks

2 yellow squash, cut into 2-inch chunks

8 ounces fresh mushrooms, cleaned

2 red and green bell peppers, cut into
2-inch chunks

2 medium red onions, cut into wedges

2 ears sweet corn, cut into
2-inch chunks

16 whole cherry tomatoes

8 ounces teriyaki sauce

Wash vegetables except mushrooms. Brush mushrooms clean. Cut vegetables to size according to recipe. Thread vegetables onto skewers. (If using wood skewers, make sure you soak them.) Place on grill over medium-hot heat. Grill 20 minutes or until tender, turning frequently.

Grilled Polenta and Radicchio

4 cups almond milk

2 garlic cloves, smashed

1 rosemary sprig

1 thyme sprig

1 cup instant polenta

Salt and freshly ground pepper

1 cup balsamic vinegar

2 medium heads radicchio, cut into
   1-inch-thick wedges through the cores

Olive oil, for drizzling and brushing

Lightly oil a 9-inch-square ceramic baking dish. In a medium saucepan, combine the almond milk, garlic, rosemary, and thyme, and bring to a boil. Remove from heat and let steep for 10 minutes. Discard the garlic, rosemary, and thyme, and return the mixture to a boil. Gradually whisk in the polenta and simmer over low heat, whisking often, until very thick and no longer gritty, 10 minutes. Season with salt and pepper. Pour the polenta into the baking dish. Let cool to room temperature, then cover and refrigerate for at least 2 hours. Meanwhile, in a small saucepan, boil the balsamic vinegar over moderately high heat until reduced to ¼ cup, about 15 minutes. Let cool to room temperature. Light a grill. Drizzle the radicchio wedges with olive oil and season with salt and pepper. Grill over moderately high heat until lightly charred and just tender, about 3 minutes per side. Clean the grill with a wire brush. Carefully unmold the polenta and cut it into 8 wedges or squares. Brush all over with olive oil. Grill the polenta until it's lightly charred on the bottom and releases easily, 4 minutes per side. Arrange the grilled polenta and radicchio on plates, drizzle with the balsamic reduction, and serve. Serves 4.

Grilled Stuffed Zucchini

4 medium zucchini

6 teaspoons olive oil, divided

1 small red onion, finely chopped

3 cloves garlic, minced

½ cup panko

1 cup shredded part-skim vegan
mozzarella cheese

1 tablespoon minced fresh mint

½ teaspoon salt

3 tablespoons grated vegan Parmesan
cheese

Cut zucchini in half lengthwise; scoop out pulp, leaving ¼-inch-thick shells. Brush with 2 teaspoons oil; set aside. Chop pulp. In a large skillet, sauté pulp and onion in remaining oil. Add garlic; cook 1 minute longer. Add panko; cook and stir for 2 minutes or until golden brown. Remove from the heat. Stir in the mozzarella cheese, mint, and salt. Spoon into zucchini shells. Sprinkle with Parmesan cheese. Grill, covered, over medium heat for 8 to 10 minutes or until zucchini is tender. Makes 4 servings.

Corn on the Cob with Chile Lime Vegan Butter

8 ears corn on the cob

½ cup vegan butter, softened

1 tablespoon honey

2 tablespoons fresh lime juice

½ teaspoon chili powder

In a small mixing bowl, cream the vegan butter with the honey, lime juice, and chili powder. Leftovers may be refrigerated, tightly covered with plastic wrap, for up to 2 weeks. Peel one side of corn husk away from cob without removing completely and loosen remaining husk. Do not remove silk. Brush butter mixture over kernels and smooth back husk to original shape. Twist open end to close. Prepare grill. Place corn directly onto coals. Cover grill with lid or foil tent. Cook 2 to 3 minutes. Test. If not done, turn and roast another 2 minutes. The outside husk will be charred. To serve, strip off husks and silk. Serves 4-8.

Party
Fare

Vegetarian Moon in the 7th House Rolls

1 tablespoon olive oil

1 teaspoon sesame oil

1 cup carrots, shredded

1 each red and yellow bell peppers, sliced

1½ cups snow peas, thinly sliced

1 cup green cabbage, shredded

1 cup kale, chopped

2 cloves garlic, minced

1 teaspoon fresh ginger, minced

¼ cup fresh cilantro, de-stemmed

2 teaspoons sake

2 teaspoons white wine vinegar

¼ cup vegetarian hoisin sauce

1 tablespoon chili sauce

1 package potsticker wrappers

1 flax egg

Peanut or sunflower oil for frying

Heat wok (or stockpot if you are wokless) over high heat until very hot. Add oil, then garlic and ginger. Cook for a minute and then add the vegetables and cook about 6 minutes more, stirring frequently. Transfer to a bowl and add sake, rice vinegar, hoisin sauce, chili sauce, and cilantro.

To make Moon Rolls, place 2 to 3 tablespoons of vegetable filling in the center of the wrapper. Using your fingers or a pastry brush, spread flax egg all around the edges. Fold in half and pinch the edges tightly. They will resemble little half-moons. Wipe the wok clean. Heat 3 cups peanut or sunflower oil on high heat. Drop egg rolls in batches of 3 and cook for 1 minute, or until golden brown. Remove with slotted spoon, place on a cookie sheet lined with paper towels to drain oil, and serve immediately with dipping sauce.

Dipping Sauce

3 cloves garlic, finely minced

1 inch fresh ginger, finely minced

½ cup apricot preserves

½ cup raspberry preserves

4 tablespoons rice vinegar (and/or sake)

In a small bowl whisk together until smooth.

Serve with: Chinese hot mustard

Everyone can create their own dipping sauce by blending the two.

Fresh Spring Rolls

4 sheets rice paper rolls

1 bunch cilantro

20 basil leaves

1 red pepper, thinly sliced

1 bunch green onions

2 carrots, thinly sliced to long ribbons

16 ounces cooked tofu, thinly sliced

1 small head red cabbage, thinly sliced to long ribbons

½ cup peanuts, chopped

Arrange equal amounts of tofu and vegetables in 4 separate piles. You will follow this procedure with each of the 4 wraps. Moisten the rice paper either by brushing a thin layer of water or simply sprinkling a little water with your fingers. The key is to make the stiff rice paper more malleable. Place cabbage in the center of the rice paper. Add the cilantro, basil leaves, red pepper, green onion, carrots, and tofu. Sprinkle the chopped peanuts over the vegetables. Fold rice paper in half, then fold over the side and roll from the bottom up. Slice the roll in half on the diagonal and serve with peanut sauce. Serves 8.

Peanut Sauce

2 cups crunchy peanut butter

½ cup fresh lime juice

½ cup fresh orange juice

¼ cup soy sauce

¼ cup rice vinegar

½ cup brown sugar

3 tablespoons crushed red pepper

2 inches fresh ginger, peeled and chopped

5 cloves garlic

1 cup coarsely chopped peanuts

½ cup fresh cilantro

Mince the garlic and ginger. In the bowl of a food processor fitted with a steel blade add the rest of the ingredients and blend until smooth. You can add less pepper if you are shy about the kick. Taste the sauce and add more soy and peppers to suit your taste. Add more orange juice for desired consistency. Add the fresh cilantro just before serving. You can either serve it warm or at room temperature.

Mediterranean Lentils with Hummus, Cucumber, Tomato, and Arugula Wrap

Whole-grain lavash bread

½ cup cooked lentils per wrap

¼ cup diced tomatoes per wrap

¼ cup diced cucumbers per wrap

Handful of arugula per wrap

Sun-Dried Tomato Hummus

1 (15-ounce) can garbanzo beans (reserve juice)

3 tablespoons sun-dried tomatoes packed in oil, chopped

4 tablespoons tahini

2 tablespoons olive oil

1 clove garlic

½ teaspoon paprika

Salt and pepper, to taste

2 tablespoons lemon juice

Reserved garbanzo juice as needed

Hummus

Place all ingredients into food processor/blender, except for the reserved garbanzo juice. Blend until creamy, about 3 minutes or so, adding the garbanzo juice as needed to thin.

ASSEMBLE YOUR WRAP

Lay your lavash bread on a flat surface. Spread a nice layer of hummus over ¾ of the bread. Top with ½ cup lentils and then the tomatoes, cucumber, and arugula. Tightly wrap at the end closest to you and then slice in half and serve. Makes 1 wrap. (Add ½ cup of wrap ingredients per person.)

Raw Pad Thai

Many natural foods markets allow you to grind your own peanut butter. If that's not an option, find a peanut butter that is as raw as possible. Another key ingredient in this dish is the kelp noodle, made from an edible brown seaweed high in iodine. Marketed as a low-calorie alternative to pasta and other noodle varieties, kelp noodles are a staple in raw and gluten-free diets. Kelp noodles are said to improve thyroid health, help protect against osteoporosis, promote weight loss and enhance heart health. Green tea kelp noodles offer the added benefits of the powerful antioxidants found in green tea.

1 12-ounce package kelp noodles or green tea kelp noodles

2 cups mustard greens

2 cups arugula

10 basil leaves, chopped

½ cup raw peanuts

½ cup green onions

Place the kelp noodles in a large bowl and toss with the sauce. Toss the arugula and mustard greens together and place on a large serving plate. Pour the dressed noodles over the greens, and garnish with basil, peanuts, and green onions. Serves 2. Can easily be doubled.

Sauce

4 tablespoons peanut butter (whole food or raw section in market)

⅓ cup coconut oil

1 tablespoon soy sauce

⅓ cup coriander seeds

2 whole Thai chili peppers (red)

Juice and zest of 1 medium lemon

½ cup water

Blend all ingredients in food processor until completely mixed.

Spicy Peanut Bun Bun *Noodles*

Peanut Noodles

1 pound dry pasta — spaghetti or angel hair (made without eggs)

2 cups peanut butter

½ cup tamari

1 teaspoon red pepper flakes

3 tablespoons toasted sesame oil

4 cloves garlic, minced

3 tablespoons sunflower oil

Garnishes

slivered carrots, green onions, red peppers, fresh cilantro, sesame seeds, and toasted peanuts

Cook pasta in large pot of boiling water. Drain the noodles, let stand and use the warm pot to make the sauce. (It helps with the thickness of the peanut butter.) Whisk the rest of the ingredients until blended. Mix in the pasta. Let stand in the refrigerator for at least 4 hours. Before serving, toss with the garnishes of your choice. Serves 6 to 8.

Kelp Noodles in Almond Butter Miso sauce

4 12-ounce packages kelp noodles

2 red bell peppers, julienned

2 green peppers, julienned

2 carrots, julienned

3 scallions, julienned

For the Sauce

1½ cups almond butter

4 teaspoons miso paste

4 tablespoons sesame oil

2-inch chunk of fresh ginger, grated

3 garlic cloves, minced

2 tablespoons apple cider vinegar

1 cup water

Combine carrots, peppers, scallions, and kelp noodles in a bowl. Reserve a little of the veggies for garnish. Set aside. In a blender or food processor, combine all of the sauce ingredients and blend until smooth. Pour the sauce over the noodle and vegetable mixture, and toss until the sauce is evenly distributed. Garnish with extra veggies and serve.

Portobello Mushrooms *in* Reduced Dark Cherry Balsamic

6 portobello mushrooms

Olive oil for brushing

Brush mushrooms with olive oil. Place on grill and weight down with a press or the flat side of a skillet. Cook about 7 minutes, flip and finish cooking for about 5 minutes. Remove from heat and cover. Serves 6.

Reduced Dark Cherry Balsamic

- 1 cup dark cherry (or fig) balsamic vinegar
- 3 tablespoons vegan butter, separated into 1-tablespoon chunks
- ¼ cup flour
- 2 tablespoons rosemary, chopped
- 6 tablespoons tomatoes, chopped

In a skillet bring dark cherry balsamic vinegar to a boil. Let reduce a bit for about 3 minutes. Using a fork, stab the first tablespoon of butter and drench in the flour. Whisk into the reduced dark cherry balsamic. Repeat with the last 2 tablespoons of butter and you will have the perfect consistency. Serves 6.

Stir-Fry Kale

2 tablespoons olive oil

1 large red onion, chopped

1 large garlic clove, chopped

1 yellow pepper, chopped

1 sprig rosemary, chopped

1½ teaspoons sea salt

½ cup basil, chopped

½ cup cilantro, chopped

1 teaspoon red pepper flakes

½ cup raw almonds

2 heads fresh kale, chopped

In a wok, heat olive oil and then add the onions. Caramelize for about 10 minutes until golden brown. Add the garlic and yellow bell pepper and continue cooking until tender, about 3 minutes longer. Add the rosemary and kale and stir-fry for 1 minute. Do not overcook; the kale should be crunchy and bright green. Season to taste with red pepper and sea salt. Top with basil, cilantro, and almonds. Serves 4.

Baked Baby Yams

Baby yams are the young, edible roots of the same plant that produces fully grown yams. The coloring of baby yams can range from deep yellow to orange flesh, while the skin on the outside is usually a pale salmon color and smooth to the touch. They have a slightly more intense flavor than the more mature yam and are in season fall and winter. If they are out of season and you cannot find them, you can substitute with any yam or sweet potato by simply slicing them in quarters.

3 pounds baby yams, washed and sliced in half

Fresh rosemary

½ cup coconut oil, melted

Sea salt

Cayenne pepper

Fresh garlic

Cover the yams in coconut oil. Season with garlic, sea salt, and cayenne pepper and let sit for 1 hour.

Preheat oven to 350°F and bake for 1 hour or until yams are soft. Serves 4.

Assorted Seasonal Vegetables *with Green Curry*

3 tablespoons olive oil

2 tablespoons green curry paste

1½ pounds assorted vegetables
(carrots, zucchini, green beans,
eggplant, peppers, winter squash)

4 kaffir lime leaves

2 lemongrass stalks, bruised and cut

2 cups unsweetened coconut milk

½ pound snow peas

15 basil leaves

You can use any assorted vegetables
that you like. Chop them in a similar size,
about 1-inch chunks. In a wok or frying
pan heat the oil. Add the green curry paste
and stir-fry until bubbly and fragrant. Add
the vegetables, kaffir lime leaves, and
lemongrass. Cook until the vegetables
are soft. Add the snow peas and cook for
another minute. Stir in the coconut milk
and bring to a gentle boil. Simmer and stir
occasionally for 5 minutes. Stir in the basil
and serve over rice.

Jambalaya

2 cups cooked brown or basmati rice

2 cups cooked pinto beans

2 cups cooked white beans

2 cups cooked black beans

1 medium onion, chopped

¼ cup roasted garlic, chopped

1 medium red pepper, chopped

1 cup chopped sweet cherry tomatoes

5 cups assorted vegetables —
cauliflower, broccoli, green beans,
carrots (anything in season)

½ cup cilantro

½ cup basil

⅓ cup rosemary

1 cup red or yellow curry sauce

1 cup sweet chili sauce

Cayenne pepper

Sea salt

In a large pot sauté the onions, garlic, and red pepper. Add tomatoes and assorted vegetables and beans. Add seasoning and sauces. Bring to a boil and let simmer for 2 hours. Add beans and rice. Serves 8.

Baked Spinach Cakes

16 ounces fresh spinach
    (1 bag or 1 large bunch),
    washed well and chopped fine
OR
16 ounces frozen spinach,
    thawed and well squeezed, drained
    of as much liquid as possible

1 cup vegan ricotta cheese

½ cup finely shredded vegan Parmesan
    cheese, plus more for garnish

2 large flax eggs, beaten (1 tablespoon
    ground flaxseed to 3 tablespoons
    water per egg)

3 cloves garlic, minced

½ teaspoon freshly grated nutmeg

Salt and freshly ground pepper, to taste

Preheat oven to 400°F. In a medium bowl
add spinach, ricotta, Parmesan, eggs,
garlic, nutmeg, salt and pepper; stir to
combine. Coat a 12-cup standard-size
muffin pan with cooking spray. Divide the
spinach mixture among the 12 cups; they
will be very full and very dense. Sprinkle
with Parmesan cheese. Bake the spinach
cakes until set, about 30 minutes. Let
stand in the pan for 5 minutes. Loosen
the edges with a knife and place on a
large serving platter. Serve warm or at
room temperature with a dollop of vegan
or plant-based sour cream or almond
yogurt. Serves 6 to 8.

Vegan Burrito

4 whole-grain tortillas

4 cups cooked black beans

4 cups cooked brown rice

1 cup vegan guacamole (recipe follows)

4 tablespoons sun-dried tomato paste

1 cup red peppers, sliced lengthwise

1 cup yellow peppers, sliced lengthwise

1 red onion, sliced lengthwise

3 cloves garlic, minced

1 jalapeño, minced

3 tablespoons olive oil

4 tablespoons each basil and cilantro, chopped

In a sauté pan heat olive oil over medium heat until just smoking. Toss in the onions and garlic and cook until tender, about 5 minutes. Add the peppers and continue sautéing for another 5 minutes and remove from heat.

For each burrito, you will lay out a tortilla and then layer in the center 1 tablespoon sun-dried tomato paste followed by ¼ cup vegan guacamole. Then layer 1 cup beans followed by 1 cup rice. Then layer ¼ of the pepper mixture. Then sprinkle with the fresh herbs. From the bottom of the tortilla fold the burrito in half. Fold the right and left side edges inside and roll from the bottom up to the top. Continue with the 3 remaining burritos. Serves 4.

Vegan Guacamole

2 large ripe avocados

¼ red onion, minced

1 clove garlic, minced

¼ cup cilantro

1 small tomato, chopped fine

Mix together to make a paste.

Cajun Grilled Eggplant

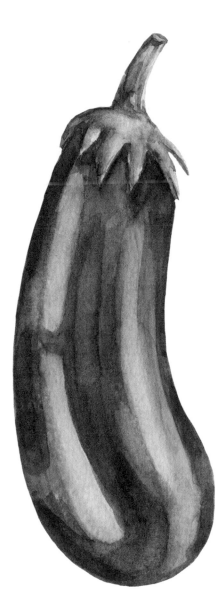

6 small (baby) eggplants

2 tablespoons paprika

2 tablespoons cayenne pepper

1 tablespoon pepper

6 cloves garlic, minced

3 tablespoons onion flakes

2 tablespoons dried oregano

Salt

Wash the eggplants and slice them in half. Mix all the seasoning ingredients together with a mortar and pestle until powdery. Rub all over the eggplant on both sides and leave for 1 or 2 hours. Heat grill until hot. Spread some oil over the eggplant filets and place on the grill, flesh side down. Cook for 5 minutes. Turn over and cook until done. Serves 4.

Noni's Zucchini Lasagna

3 pounds zucchini, scrubbed

5 cups tomato sauce

2 pounds ricotta cashew cheese (recipe follows)

4 cups spinach, finely chopped

2 tablespoons parsley, chopped

½ teaspoon each dried oregano, basil, and nutmeg

Salt and pepper, to taste

1 cup nutritional yeast

1 pound vegan mozzarella cheese (recipe follows)

Slice zucchini into long slices. Cook in boiling water just until limp, about 5 minutes. Drain on paper towels. Combine ricotta, spinach, parsley, seasoning, and half of the nutritional yeast in a bowl. Set aside. In a 9×13 pan, spoon a thin layer of tomato sauce. Arrange layer of zucchini over this. Spoon half of the reserved ricotta mixture on top of the zucchini. Sprinkle with half the mozzarella cheese. Arrange the rest of the zucchini over this, layer more tomato sauce and top with remaining ricotta mixture. Top with remaining mozzarella and parmesan. Bake in a 350°F oven for about 1 hour or until top is brown. Let stand 10 minutes before cutting. Serves 8.

Ricotta Cashew Cheese

- 1½ cups raw cashews
- 1 lemon, juice and zest
- 3 tablespoons nutritional yeast
- ½ teaspoon sea salt, to taste
- Combination of fresh herbs: oregano, thyme, basil, rosemary

Place the cashews in a bowl and add several cups of filtered water. Let them soak overnight. This will soften the cashews and make them creamier and easier to process. Drain the cashews and place them in the bowl of a food processor. Add the lemon juice, zest, salt, and nutritional yeast, and process for about a minute. In order to make the cheese as creamy as possible, stop the food processor occasionally and scrape down the sides. Continue processing until the mixture becomes creamy and starts to hold together, almost with the same consistency as ricotta cheese. Add in your combination of fresh herbs. Makes about 2 cups.

Vegan Mozzarella

- 1 cup unsweetened non-dairy yogurt
- ½ cup water
- ⅓ cup grapeseed oil
- 1 tablespoon salt
- 6 tablespoons tapioca flour
- 1 tablespoon carrageenan powder
- ½ teaspoon xanthan gum
- 8 cups ice water

Place yogurt, water, oil, and 1 teaspoon salt in a blender. Process about 3 minutes until smooth and creamy, stopping after each minute to scrape down the sides. Transfer to a clean glass bowl, cover and let rest at room temperature for 24 hours. Transfer to a heavy pot and thicken with tapioca flour, carrageenan and xanthan gum. Stir constantly with a whisk over medium heat until thick and gooey, about 5 minutes. To make the brine place the ice water and the rest of the salt in a pan and stir until dissolved. Using a small ice cream scoop, form balls and drop into the brine. Cover and refrigerate for up to 1 week.

Vegan *Pizza*

Pizza Dough

1 cup warm water

1 packet fast-acting yeast

2 cups all-purpose flour

2 tablespoons olive oil (+ more for
    seasoning crust)

2 tablespoons sugar, divided

1 teaspoon salt (+ more for crust)

Toppings

½ cup marinara sauce

plant-based mozzarella (recipe above),
    sliced

½ cup fresh basil, chopped

½ teaspoon fresh thyme

Preheat oven to 500°F. Stir yeast and ½
tablespoon sugar into warmed water until
dissolved. Let it sit for 5 minutes, until
foamy. In a large bowl, add the flour, salt,
and remaining sugar. Whisk to combine.
Add the activated yeast to the bowl along
with the olive oil. Mix until all ingredients
are well combined and form a dough.
If dough is too sticky, add a couple
tablespoons of flour. Form the dough
into a ball and place back in the bowl.
Completely cover the bowl with a damp
napkin or hand towel for 30 minutes or
until dough doubles in size.

Using a large cookie sheet or pizza pan, place a large piece of parchment paper over your work area (about the size of your pan). Dust the paper with flour so you can spread your dough easily. Cut the dough in half using a wet knife. Using your hands, spread dough across the parchment paper into a round pizza shape to your desired thickness. The edges should be slightly thicker to form a pillowed crust. To season your crust, lightly brush with olive oil and sprinkle with salt. Using a spoon, spread the sauce evenly over the pizza and top with the mozzarella. Carefully slide the parchment paper onto your pan to transfer to the oven. Now slide the parchment paper back off your pan and directly onto the middle oven rack. Bake for 10 to 15 minutes, until the crust is golden brown. Slice and serve. Makes two 10-inch pizzas.

Apple Pie Oatmeal Cookies

4 teaspoons ground flaxseed

½ cup warm water

4 cups regular or quick-cooking oats

1 teaspoon baking soda

½ teaspoon salt

1 teaspoon cinnamon

½ teaspoon allspice

½ teaspoon ground ginger

½ teaspoon nutmeg

½ teaspoon ground cloves

2 large apples, peeled, cored and chopped

4 ounces pitted and chopped dates (about 8 medjool dates or ½ cup packed chopped dates)

¼ cup water

2 teaspoons apple cider vinegar

Preheat oven to 350°F. In a small bowl whisk together the ground flaxseed with the warm water and set aside until thickened. In a bowl mix oats, baking soda, and spices. Place the apple, dates, ¼ cup water, and apple cider vinegar in the blender. Blend until it's about the consistency of applesauce. Pour it into the oat mixture, then add the flaxseed and stir to combine. Drop by rounded tablespoons onto a baking sheet lined with parchment paper. Flatten each cookie slightly with a fork. Bake for about 12 minutes. Cool on a wire rack before serving. Makes about 2 dozen cookies.

Strawberry Margarita Pie

Crust

16 graham crackers, crushed

3 tablespoons sugar

1 cup vegan butter

Mix the ingredients and press them into a 9-inch pie plate. Bake in a preheated 350°F oven for 10 to 12 minutes until lightly browned. Place on a rack to cool.

Pie

12 tablespoons ground golden flaxseed

2¼ cups water

1 pint strawberries

2 tablespoons sugar

1 teaspoon orange zest, orange portion only

1¾ cups full-fat coconut cream

½ cup xylitol

½ cup fresh key lime juice (approximately 12 key limes)

2 teaspoons grated lime peel, green portion only

WHIPPED CREAM FOR GARNISH

½ cup full-fat coconut cream

2 teaspoons xylitol

¼ teaspoon vanilla

Place strawberries, 2 tablespoons of sugar, and the orange zest in a saucepan. Mix over low heat stirring constantly until soft, about 15 minutes. Let cool for a few minutes and blend with an immersion blender, leaving chunky. In a stand mixer beat together the flaxseed and water. Turn the mixer off and add the coconut cream. Turn speed to low and mix in half of the lime juice. Once the juice is incorporated, add the other half of the juice and the zest; continue to mix until blended. Mix in the strawberry mixture and continue to mix until just blended, about 1 minute. Pour the mixture into the pie shell and bake at 350°F for 20 minutes. Let cool completely. Meanwhile in a clean bowl of an electric mixer beat the coconut cream, xylitol, and vanilla. Place in pastry bag with a star tip and pipe around the edges of the pie. Sprinkle with grated lime zest and chill for at least 2 hours before serving.

Emma's Matcha Green Tea Ice Cream

4 cups unsweetened almond milk

2 cups coconut creamer

½ cup xylitol

½ cup brown rice syrup

10 tablespoons matcha green tea powder

3 teaspoons vanilla

Dash of salt

Place all ingredients in a blender and puree. Chill overnight in the refrigerator. Follow the instructions on your ice cream maker. Allow it to spin for 30 minutes. It will be soft so it will need to be in the freezer for a few hours, or overnight is best. Serves 4 to 6.

Raw Blueberry Almond Dark Chocolate Bark

3 cups 60–80% vegan dark chocolate (or chocolate chips), broken into large pieces

1 tablespoon vanilla

1 teaspoon Grand Marnier (optional)

1 cup sliced almonds, lightly toasted

1 cup dried blueberries

Zest of 1 large orange

Line a baking sheet with parchment paper. Melt chocolate, vanilla, and Grand Marnier if using, on the top of a double boiler. Stir and push down sides with a silicone spatula. Pour the chocolate onto the parchment paper, and spread with the spatula to create a rectangle. Press in the almonds and blueberries and sprinkle on the zest. Refrigerate until hard, then break into pieces and store in an airtight container.

Rice Pudding with Whipped Cashew Cream

4 cups water

2 cups brown rice, rinsed

2½ cups rice milk

1 cup currants

⅔ cup brown rice syrup

2 teaspoons vanilla

1 teaspoon cinnamon

½ teaspoon ground ginger

¼ teaspoon ground nutmeg

Place the water and rice into a medium saucepan and bring to a boil. Cover and reduce the heat to low, and simmer for 35 minutes or until all of the water has been absorbed. Add the remaining ingredients, stir well to combine, and continue to cook the mixture over low heat until all of the liquid has been absorbed. Transfer the mixture to a bowl and place the pudding in the refrigerator to chill overnight.

Sweet Cashew Whipped Cream

3 cups cashews, soaked in water overnight

¼ to ½ cup water

2 tablespoons maple syrup

1 tablespoon vanilla

Drain the cashews. Place all ingredients in blender and pulse until light, smooth and fluffy. Place in a bowl and let refrigerate overnight to thicken a bit. To serve, place the pudding into 10 bowls. Spoon the cashew whipped cream over the top. Sprinkle with cinnamon.

Raw Apricot Sorbet

6 cups fresh apricots, pitted

3 tablespoons raw honey

¼ cup lime juice

Cut the apricots into small pieces and place in a food processor. Add honey and lime juice. Blend until smooth. Churn in an ice cream maker according to the manufacturer's instructions. Once churned, transfer to an airtight container and freeze for 2 hours or overnight before serving. Serves 4 to 6.

Baked Pear, Cranberry, and Apple

4 pears, chopped

4 apples, chopped

1 cup dried cranberries

½ cup agave nectar

½ teaspoon cinnamon

½ teaspoon Chinese Five Spice

Topping

1 cup quick-cooking oatmeal

1 cup chopped nuts

In a square glass pan toss together apples, pears, cranberry, agave, and spices. In a bowl mix the oatmeal and nuts. Sprinkle over the fruit mixture and bake in a preheated 350°F oven for about 40 minutes until bubbly. Serves 6 to 8.

Grandma Kay's Zucchini Bread

1 cup vegetable oil

1 cup brown sugar

3 flax eggs (3 tablespoons ground
    flaxseeds mixed with 9 tablespoons
    water)

1 tablespoon pure vanilla extract

2 cups grated zucchini

3 cups flour

1 teaspoon cinnamon

1 teaspoon salt

1 teaspoon baking powder

½ teaspoon baking soda

1 cup coarsely chopped walnuts

1 cup raisins or dried cranberries

Preheat oven to 325°F. Oil two 5x9 loaf pans. In a large bowl, combine the oil and brown sugar. Add the eggs one at a time, beating after every addition. Stir in the vanilla and zucchini. In a smaller bowl, sift together flour, cinnamon, salt, baking powder and soda. Stir the dry ingredients into the oil and egg mixture until just moistened. Fold in the raisins and walnuts. Spoon batter into the prepared loaf pans. Bake for about 1 hour, until a knife in the center comes out clean. Makes 2 loaves.

Vegan Brownies

1 cup coconut oil

2 cups 60% cacao bittersweet chocolate baking chips

1 tablespoon vanilla

1 cup water

1 cup xylitol

1 cup pastry flour

1 cup whole wheat flour

1 cup Dutch process cocoa (60% cacao or higher)

1 teaspoon baking powder

1 teaspoon baking soda

1 teaspoon salt

3 tablespoons ground flaxseed

1 tablespoon cornstarch

½ cup hot water

Preheat oven to 350°F and grease a 9x13 pan with coconut oil. In a double boiler or a bowl set atop a pot of gently simmering water, melt the coconut oil, ½ of the chocolate chips, and vanilla together. When melted add the xylitol and remove from heat. In another bowl, whisk together the flours, cocoa, baking powder, baking soda, and salt. In another bowl, whisk together the flaxseed, cornstarch and ½ cup hot water; allow to sit for 5 minutes. Combine the chocolate/coconut oil mixture with the flaxseed mixture and whisk vigorously. Add to the flour mixture and stir to incorporate. Add the other half of the chocolate chips and mix well. Pour the batter into the greased baking pan and bake for about 50 minutes. Start checking the brownies after the first 30 minutes to ensure they are baking evenly, and turn the pan around in the oven. When cooked soft and cake-like to the touch, remove from the oven and let cool completely before cutting. Makes 20 squares.

Lotus Kitchen Cookie

4 cups almond meal

½ teaspoon sea salt

½ teaspoon baking soda

1 teaspoon cinnamon

¾ cup coconut oil, melted

½ cup maple syrup

2 tablespoons vanilla

1 cup dark chocolate, chopped

½ cup dried cranberries

½ cup candied ginger

Preheat oven to 350°F. Mix the almond meal, salt, baking soda, and cinnamon. Stir in the coconut oil, maple syrup, and vanilla. Stir in the chopped chocolate, cranberry, and ginger. Drop by rounded tablespoon onto ungreased baking sheets. Bake for 10 to 12 minutes on parchment paper-lined cookie sheet (the edges should be golden). Let them sit on the pan for 5 to 10 minutes. They firm up during this time, so this is an important step. Remove and enjoy. Makes 3 dozen.

Crispy Rice Treats

1 cup vegan butter

2 cups vegan marshmallows (recipe follows)

1 teaspoon vanilla

8 cups crispy rice cereal

Line a 9x13-inch baking pan with parchment paper and lightly brush with sunflower oil. Set aside. In a large pot, melt the vegan butter. Add the vegan marshmallows and stir, until the marshmallows are melted. Remove pan from heat and stir in the vanilla. Fold in the cereal using a large spoon or spatula. There will be chunks of marshmallows and that's okay, just try to coat all the crispy rice. Transfer to the prepared pan and press down evenly either with your hands or a spatula. You can lightly grease the spatula if it sticks. Place in freezer for 10 minutes while you make the peanut butter drizzle.

Peanut Butter Drizzle

2 tablespoons creamy peanut butter

1 teaspoon maple syrup

1 to 2 teaspoons water, to thin, if needed

Fill a small pot halfway with water. Using a metal bowl that fits over the pot, melt the peanut butter and maple syrup. Add water 1 teaspoon at a time to thin out as needed.

Remove the treats from the freezer and drizzle with the peanut mixture. Let set out for 3 hours, then cut and serve. Place in an airtight container for 2 weeks. Makes 18 squares.

Vegan Marshmallows

Sunflower oil, to grease the pan

1½ cups powdered sugar

½ cup cornstarch

¾ cup cold water

1½ cups granulated sugar

1½ cups corn syrup

3 tablespoons agar agar powder

Pinch salt

Candy thermometer

Grease bottom and sides of an 8x8 pan. In a small bowl, combine powdered sugar and cornstarch. Use a few spoonfuls of the mixture to coat the pan on all sides and corners. Set the pan aside and save the remainder of the mixture until your marshmallows are completely set and ready to cut. In a 4-quart, heavy-bottomed saucepan, pour in ¾ cup water. On top of the water, pour the granulated sugar, corn syrup, agar agar powder, and a pinch of salt. Give 1 or 2 very quick stirs. Bring to a rapid boil until the mixture has reached a temperature of 214–220°F. This takes at least 15 minutes or so, but you want to keep a watchful eye. Once the sugar mixture has come to temperature, remove from heat. Turn your stand mixer, fitted with the whisk attachment, on to low, and very carefully and slowly pour hot syrup down the side of the bowl while the mixer is on low. Once all liquid is in the bowl, gradually turn up to high. Whip the mixture for 10 minutes until it is thick and forms ribbons when you pull up the whisk. Immediately transfer the whipped mixture to the prepared 8x8 pan and spoon it evenly. Let it set out for 12 to 18 hours, uncovered. When they are completely dry, cut into squares. Toss in the remaining powdered sugar/cornstarch mixture so it is coated on all sides. Keeps up to 2 weeks in an airtight container.

Papa's Chocolate Avocado Pudding

2 large ripe avocados, peeled and sliced

2 ripe bananas

½ cup unsweetened cocoa powder

½ cup raw sugar

⅓ cup almond, cashew, coconut, or hemp milk

2 teaspoons vanilla

Pinch of ground cinnamon

Pinch of ground turmeric

Blend avocados, bananas, cocoa powder, sugar, milk, vanilla extract, cinnamon, and turmeric in a blender or food processor until smooth. Refrigerate pudding until chilled, about 30 minutes. Serves 4.

Triple Berry Chia Pudding

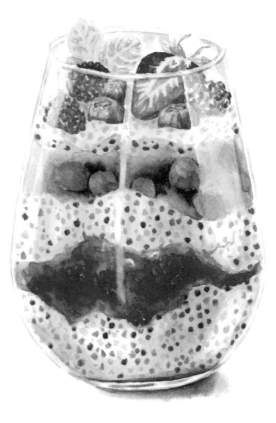

2 cups full-fat coconut cream

3 tablespoons maple syrup

1 teaspoon vanilla

½ cup chia seed

1 cup blueberries

1 cup raspberries

Blueberries, raspberry, blackberries,
   strawberries, mint for garnish

In a bowl whisk together coconut cream, maple syrup, vanilla, and chia seeds. In the bowl of a food processor fitted with a steel blade separately puree the blueberries, then the raspberries. Place in separate work bowls. Mix ⅓ of the chia mixture with the blueberries. Mix ⅓ with the raspberries. Using 6 parfait cups, layer starting with the plain mixture, followed with the blueberry mixture, finishing with raspberry. Place in the refrigerator for 2 hours. Garnish with the extra berries and mint. You can also layer in a trifle dish and garnish in the same way. Serves 6.

Acknowledgments

An Abundance of Gratitude

Emma Rose Mackenzie, thank you for stretching me in ways I never knew were possible both professionally and personally. I love you so.

My friends and family who are always gathered around my table having stimulating conversation and enjoying great food. Maybe a few fails, but you are always kind.

Back to The Kitchen Catering crew and clients, you always keep me creative and inspired.

Team Huqua Press, so grateful to you all. In particular Bill Smith and Dave Shulman (the not-so-simple designSimple dynamic duo), Shelley Waldenmeyer Ferrer, Laura Smith and Paulina "Pina" Palacios.

To Alice Waters, The Edible Schoolyard Project and Larchmont Charter. A big shout-out to everyone who is feeding kids real food and teaching sustainability.

Thank you you to the team of watercolorists—you took the ordinary and made it extraordinary. I will forever see vegetables and fruit as art.

And finally, Judy Proffer. You are a publisher extraordinaire. I adore you and am thrilled to have co-created this with you. Thank you for all your love, honesty, and trust.